The Crafter's Design Library

Celebrations

Sharon Bennett

David and Charles

...and Libby & Sophie, this is for you x x x

A DAVID & CHARLES BOOK
Copyright © David & Charles Limited 2006

David & Charles is an F+W Publications Inc. company
4700 East Galbraith Road
Cincinnati, OH 45236

First published in the UK in 2006
First paperback edition 2006

Text and illustrations copyright © Sharon Bennett 2006

Sharon Bennett has asserted her right to be identified as author of this work in accordance with the
Copyright, Designs and Patents Act, 1988.

A catalogue record for this book is available from the British Library.

ISBN-13: 978-0-7153-2247-5 hardback
ISBN-10: 0-7153-2247-8 hardback

ISBN-13: 978-0-7153-2249-9 paperback
ISBN-10: 0-7153-2249-4 paperback

Printed in Singapore by KHL
for David & Charles
Brunel House   Newton Abbot   Devon

Commissioning Editor Fiona Eaton
Editor Jennifer Proverbs
Editorial Assistant Louise Clark
Designer Louise Prentice
Production Controller Beverley Richardson

Visit our website at www.davidandcharles.co.uk

David & Charles books are available from all good bookshops; alternatively you can contact
our Orderline on 0870 9908222 or write to us at FREEPOST EX2 110, D&C Direct, Newton Abbot,
TQ12 4ZZ (no stamp required UK only); US customers call 800-289-0963 and Canadian customers
call 800-840-5220.

contents

the essential techniques

Introducing celebratory art 4
Applying motifs to craft media 6
Adapting and combining designs 12
Techniques and mediums 14
Choosing a medium 18
Project gallery 20

the templates

Early Years 28
Family and Friends 42
Celebrate the Year 60
Romantic Occasions 80
Congratulations 94
Finishing Touches 108

Index 120
About the author 121

Introducing Celebratory art

Celebrations of all kinds unleash our creativity, motivating us to make something unique for our loved ones that can be treasured forever. Births, weddings and special anniversaries in particular draw our attention, but there are other events that occur every year, such as Christmas, birthdays, Valentine's Day, and so on that we also want to celebrate. For any of these occasions it can be difficult to find that special motif to feature on a handmade card, decorated bowl, painted scarf or other item that we wish to create to mark the occasion. That's where this book comes in. It's packed full of images ranging from simple outline drawings to more complicated motifs that you can use in your designs, and there are borders and corner motifs to help you add that final flourish.

The book begins with some basic information about using the templates, and you'll find this invaluable if you need a little help getting started. It includes advice on using the templates (pages 6–17) and choosing a medium (pages 18–19) and there's also an inspirational project gallery on pages 20–25, displaying items decorated using the templates from this book.

When you are ready to begin you'll find the templates you need on pages 29–119. These are supplied as simple outline drawings, which are easy to trace off and use. Because there are so many motifs to choose from they have been grouped by subject, but these are just my suggestions, so don't feel that you have to use a motif from a certain section for a particular event – let your own imagination dictate your choice.

The templates begin with the Early Years (page 28) when we celebrate those important 'firsts': first day, first haircut, first tooth, first steps and so on. This section includes a host of motifs to delight any infant or toddler. This is followed by a feast of family images that have been carefully put together to suit all those occasions involving

family and friends, from simple thank-you cards to birthdays (see page 42).

The many annual festivals we celebrate are presented in their own group and include New Year, Chinese New Year, Hanukkah, Easter, Mother's Day, Father's Day, Thanksgiving, Diwali and Christmas. This chapter is called Celebrate the Year (see page 60) and comprises of images suitable for all these holidays and more.

For those romantic occasions including Valentine's Day, engagements and weddings take a look in Romantic Occasions (page 80) where you will find a range of lovely hearts, bows, trinkets, jewellery and other motifs that will help to express your heartfelt wishes. This is then followed by Congratulations (page 94), which celebrates the passing of exams,

retirement and sporting achievements, as well as the simpler achievements of life. You'll also find motifs suitable for a good-luck card to anticipate any of these events.

Corner motifs, borders, twirls and curls are provided in the final chapter, Finishing Touches, on page 108. These can be used to enhance the other images you've chosen, or you can combine them with wording, or even use them alone for a simple but elegant effect. All in all, this extensive selection of templates should enable you to complete countless projects with ease.

The designs shown here can be found in the templates section of this book. They are all versatile designs that could be used for a host of applications. See the Project Gallery, pages 20–25 for further inspiration and advice.

Applying motifs to craft media

The techniques best suited to applying your selected motif to a particular medium depend on the surface you are working with. The following pages offer some simple advice on how to do this for the most popular craft media. Guidance is also given on how to enlarge or reduce the motif to suit your requirements (below) and how to create a stencil (page 11).

Enlarging and reducing a motif

Here are three ways to change the size of a motif to suit your project: the traditional method using a grid, or the modern alternatives of a photocopier or scanner.

Using a grid

The traditional method of enlargement involves using a grid. To begin, use low-tack masking tape to secure tracing paper over the original design. Draw a square or rectangle onto the tracing paper, enclosing the image (see below). Use a ruler to divide up the square or rectangle into rows of equally spaced vertical and horizontal lines. Complex designs should have lines about 1cm (³⁄₈in) apart; simpler ones can have lines 4cm (1½in) apart.

Now draw a square or rectangle to match your required design size, and draw a grid to correspond with the one you have just drawn over the image, as shown below. You can now begin to re-create the original image by redrawing it, square by square, at the required scale.

Using a photocopier

For fast and accurate results, use a photocopier to enlarge or reduce a motif. To do this, you need to calculate your enlargement percentage. First measure the width of the image you want to end up with. Here, the motif needs to be enlarged to 120mm (4¾in). Measure the width of the original motif, which in this case is 80mm (3¼in). Divide the first measurement by the second to find the percentage by which you need to enlarge the motif, in this instance 150%. (An enlargement must always be more than 100% and a reduction less than 100%).

To photocopy an image onto tracing paper, use tracing paper that is at least 90gsm. When photocopying an image from tracing paper, place the tracing paper onto the glass, and then lay a sheet of white paper on top of it. This will help to produce a sharp copy.

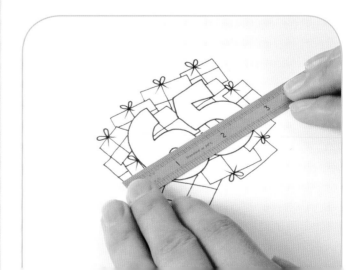

Transferring a motif onto paper, card, wood or fine fabric

A light box makes it easy to trace an image directly onto a piece of paper, thin card or fabric, but if you don't have one it is easy to improvize with household items. Balance a piece of clear plastic across two piles of books or pieces of furniture, and place a table lamp underneath. Place your motif on the plastic and your paper, thin card or fabric on top. Switch on the light and simply trace over the design showing through.

To transfer a design onto wood, thick card or foam, trace the design onto tracing paper using a sharp pencil. Turn the tracing over and redraw on the wrong side with a soft lead pencil. Now turn the tracing over again and use masking tape to secure it right side up onto your chosen surface. Carefully redraw the image – press firmly enough to transfer the motif, but take care not to damage the surface.

Using a scanner

A third way to enlarge or reduce a motif is to scan the original image on a flatbed scanner or to photograph it with a digital camera. Once the image is on your computer you can either adjust the size using image manipulation software or simply alter the percentage of your printout size. If the finished result is larger than the printer's capacity, some software will allow you to tile the image over several sheets of paper, which can then be joined together to form the whole image.

An image manipulation package may also allow you to alter the proportions of a motif, making it wider or narrower, for example. Take care not to distort it beyond recognition, though. Once you are happy with your image, it can be saved to be used again and again.

Transferring a motif onto foil

To emboss foil, simply take the original tracing and secure it to the foil surface. Rest the foil on kitchen paper. Use an embossing tool or an old ballpoint pen that has run out of ink to press down on the tracing, embossing the metal below. Use the same technique on the back of the foil to produce a raised effect.

Transferring a motif onto mirror and ceramic

Trace the motif onto tracing paper, then turn the tracing over and redraw on the wrong side using a chinagraph pencil. A chinagraph produces a waxy line that adheres well to shiny surfaces such as coloured glass, mirrored glass and ceramic. Chinagraphs are prone to blunt quickly, but it doesn't matter if the lines are thick and heavy at this stage. Use masking tape to secure the tracing right side up onto the surface. Carefully redraw with a sharp pencil to transfer the image.

Tracing a motif onto glass and acetate

Roughly cut out the motif and tape it to the underside of the acetate or glass with masking tape. It is helpful to rest glassware on a few sheets of kitchen towel for protection and to stop curved objects from rolling. The image will now show through the clear surface, and you can simply trace along the lines with glass outliner or paint directly onto the surface.

If you want to transfer an image onto opaque glass, or onto a container that is difficult to slip a motif behind, such as a bottle with a narrow neck, follow the instructions on page 7 for transferring a motif onto mirror and ceramic.

Transferring a motif onto curved items

Motifs can be transferred onto rounded items, but will need to be adapted to fit the curves. First trace the motif, redrawing it on the underside (use a chinagraph pencil if the container is ceramic). Make cuts in the template from the edge towards the centre. Lay the motif against the surface so that the cuts slightly overlap or spread open, depending on whether the surface is concave or convex. Tape the motif in place with masking tape and transfer the design by drawing over the lines with a sharp pencil.

Making a template for a plate

1 Cut a square of tracing paper slightly larger than the diameter of the plate. Make a straight cut from one edge to the centre of the paper. Place the paper centrally on the plate or saucer and tape one cut edge across the rim. Roughly cut out a circle from the centre of the paper to help it lie flat. Smooth the paper around the rim and tape in place, overlapping the cut edges. Mark the position of the overlap on the paper.

2 Turn the plate over and draw around the circumference onto the underside of the tracing paper. Remove the paper, then measure the depth of the plate rim and mark it on the paper by measuring in from the circumference. Join the marks with a curved line.

Making a template for a straight-sided container

If you wish to apply a continuous motif such as a border to a straight-sided container, make a template of the container first. To do this, slip a piece of tracing paper into a transparent glass container or around an opaque glass or ceramic container. Lay the paper smoothly against the surface and tape in place with masking tape. Mark the position of the upper edge of the container with a pencil. Now mark the position of the overlapping ends of the paper or mark each side of the handle on a mug, cup or jug.

Remove the tracing and join the overlap marks, if you have made these. Measure down from the upper edge and mark the upper limit of the band or border on the template. Cut out the template and slip it into or around the container again to check the fit. Transfer your chosen template onto the tracing paper, then onto the container.

Transferring a motif onto fabric

If fabric is lightweight and pale in colour, it may be possible to trace the motif simply by laying the fabric on top. If the fabric is dark or thick, it may help to use a light box. Place the motif under the fabric on the surface of the light box (see page 7 for information on constructing a home light box). As the light shines up through the motif and fabric you should be able to see the design lines, ready for tracing.

Alternatively, place a piece of dressmaker's carbon paper face down on the fabric and tape the motif on top with masking tape. Trace the design with a sharp pencil to transfer it onto the fabric as shown below. The marks made by the carbon are easily wiped away.

Transferring a motif onto a knitting chart

Use knitting-chart paper rather than ordinary graph paper to chart a knitting design. (Knitted stitches are wider than they are tall and knitting chart paper is sized accordingly.) Transfer the motif straight onto the knitting graph paper (see page 7 for advice on transferring onto paper). Each square on the graph paper represents a stitch. Make sure that you are happy with the number of squares in the motif, as this dictates the number of stitches in your design, and ultimately the design size. Fill in the applicable squares on the chart using appropriate coloured pens or pencils.

Use the finished chart in conjunction with a knitting pattern. Read the chart from right to left for a knit row and from left to right for a purl row. The motif can also be worked on a ready-knitted item with Swiss darning.

Transferring a motif onto needlepoint canvas and cross stitch fabric

Designs on needlepoint canvas and cross stitch fabric can be worked either by referring to the design on a chart, or by transferring the image to the material and stitching over it.

To transfer the motif onto a chart

Transfer the motif straight onto graph paper (see page 7 for advice on transferring onto paper). Each square on the graph paper represents a square of canvas mesh or Aida cross stitch fabric. Colour in the squares that the motif lines cross with coloured pencils or pens. You may want to make half stitches where the motif outline runs through a box. Mark the centre of the design along a vertical and horizontal line (see right) and mark the centre of the fabric lengthways and widthways with tacking stitches.

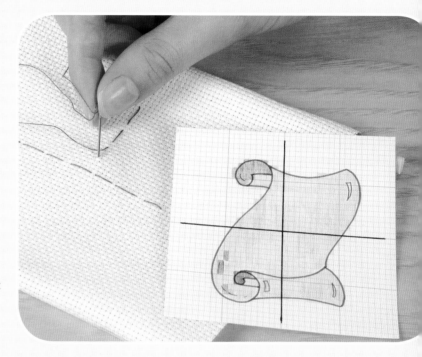

To transfer the motif directly onto canvas or fabric

With an open-weave canvas or pale fabric it is possible to trace the design directly onto the canvas or fabric. First, mark a small cross centrally on the motif and on the material. On a lightbox (see page 7), place the material on top of the motif, aligning the crosses. Tape in position and trace the image with a waterproof pen. Alternatively, use dressmaker's carbon paper to transfer the design, as explained in transferring a motif onto fabric, opposite.

Making a stencil

Tape a piece of tracing paper over the motif to be adapted into a stencil. Redraw the image, thickening the lines and creating 'bridges' between the sections to be cut out. You may find it helpful to shade in the areas to be cut out. Lay a piece of carbon paper, ink side down, on a stencil sheet, place the tracing on top, right side up, and tape in place. Redraw the design to transfer it to the stencil sheet. Finally, lay the stencil sheet on a cutting mat and carefully cut out the stencil with a craft knife, always drawing the sharp edge of the blade away from you.

Adapting and combining designs

Although you can use the templates in this book exactly as they are, a lot of fun can be had simply messing around with them, simplifying the designs, making them more ornate, combining different motifs and so on. You can do this endlessly, making your library of templates never-ending as your ideas become new images.

Simplifying an image

Sometimes the simplest images work best. This might mean removing all detail and filling in the overall shape to create a silhouette for dramatic effect. Alternatively, you might wish to remove just some of the details, either because you are using a chunky medium not suitable for detailed work or because you simply want a plainer effect, as on this horseshoe (see page 89).

Replace existing decorations with your own ideas. On the horseshoe shown here, for example, you could remove the pattern and use the words 'good luck' instead.

Repeating an image

Images that have an obvious direction work really well when flipped and repeated. This bird (page 53) creates a nice border for a card or place name card when flipped. Notice how on the lower border the bird has been omitted for a simple, stylish effect.

If you are feeling adventurous, combine two or more motifs, then flip and repeat your whole new design.

Flip and overlap

Think about overlapping images or about flipping an image and overlapping it on itself. This works well with simple motifs, such as the champagne glass from page 61, which I have turned into a silhouette and flipped on itself – ideal to celebrate the union of two people. In a second version I used the star from the same page as a background motif.

Variations on a theme

These images show how you can create four different borders from just part of the heart sash motif on page 113. Some of the original motif has been removed and the remaining image copied, flipped and rotated in a variety of ways to provide the final borders. These are ideal for card making or for painting on ceramic items such as a teapot or jug. All the templates can be enlarged or reduced in size as required.

Try using this as a border for scrapbook images or to highlight a message of good wishes.

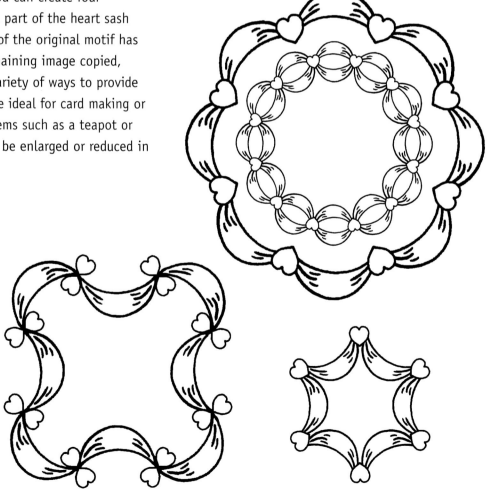

Techniques and mediums

This book covers a huge selection of motifs and it would be impossible to cover all your options for using them in these pages, but here are some ideas that cover most crafting needs.

Embossing onto metal and foil

Tracing over a design onto metal or foil sheets with an embossing tool will produce a depressed line on the side that is uppermost and a raised line on the underneath. Even the simplest of images, such as this vase from page 53, will look great on cards or labels and they can be painted for further embellishment, if desired.

Embossing works well on vellum, which looks fantastic on cards and for scrapbooking. See the Project Gallery, page 20.

Stencils

Stencils can be cut in acetate or stencil film using a craft knife, but for large images you'll find a hot cutter is easiest. With a stencil you can produce a repeat image quickly on practically anything from paper to ceramics, glass or fabrics. Hold the stencil in place with tape or spray glue and use a stencil brush to dab on the paint. Experiment with how you apply the paint as sometimes just applying it around the edges of the template gives a really delicate feel. Also colours can be added over each other, producing quite interesting effects. The cake image shown here is provided on page 50.

Decorative papers

With such a variety of excellent craft papers available for card making and paper sculpting, the possibilities for the crafter are endless. Simple images can produce very effective results and paper is brought to life by overlapping it or adding a few simple folds or curls. The use of shaped cutters, scissors or punches plus decorative pens or glitter glues provide even further creative possibilities. This pretty handbag motif is provided on page 44.

Fabric paints

You can paint or dye any natural fabric and some synthetics for a variety of lovely effects provided you use the right product for your chosen material. Cottons and linens can be painted with fabric paints, used for this rabbit design, or with pens, crayons or sprays, but silk is in a category all of its own. Silk paint spreads over the fabric with amazing speed and needs to be contained by a raised outline drawing in gutta that defines each colour area. This works particularly well with flowers and hearts and the painted fabric can be used for cards or turned into attractive handkerchiefs, cushions, scarves, ties, costumes or even curtains.

Découpage

This lovely and popular craft involves cutting out and sticking down paper motifs, often cut from gift wrap. Experiment with other papers, avoiding very thick types, which are the most difficult to finish effectively (see the tip below). Try tracing suitable designs onto paper, painting them and then colour photocopying them onto thin paper. Then all you have to do is cut them out and stick them to a painted item. Apply several protective coats of varnish to finish. This motif can be found on page 85.

Thin papers, such as tissue paper, work best for découpage and you can photocopy onto them for some lovely results.

Reversing out

'Reversing out' from a coloured background to leave a white image can give a dramatic effect, as seen on this Halloween castle (see page 71). Use a solid colour to paint the background around the design or use a paint technique, such as stippling. I dabbed off the excess paint before it dried to give an antique look. If desired you can reinforce the shape with white paint. On silk you can reverse out by applying a clear gutta to the design lines and then painting around the shapes instead of in them. On paper or ceramic, you can use a masking fluid that should be removed when the paint is dry to reveal the reversed out image.

Tonal images

Using just one colour in a design emphasizes the shape and form. In watercolour or acrylic you can do this by building up layers of a single wash or by diluting the wash to make a lighter and lighter tint. With drawing tools such as coloured pencils you may need to purchase two or three shades of the same colour. This technique works really well with geometrical designs, but also in figurative work. This motif was can be found on page 47.

Outliners

Outline pens have paint in a tube with a nozzle that pipes a line as you draw around an image, giving a raised effect. Gold is a favourite for this technique although it is available in all sorts of colours and with different properties such as pearlized or glossy. As can be seen from these balls of wool, you can achieve great results for card making (see page 51). Outliners are also manufactured to use on porcelain or glass, although these need baking to make them permanent.

Outliners can be used to make lovely 'brailed' cards and gift tags. You can use them to write messages too, and children will love tracing over their name with a finger.

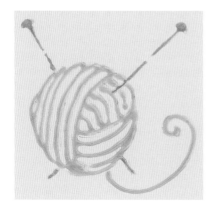
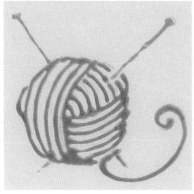

Choosing a medium

If you are painting on ceramics or fabrics your choice of medium is dictated by what is specifically designed for that product, but when working with paper or card there are many ranges at your disposal. Here some of the most versatile and readily available.

Metallic and pearlized paints

Metallic and pearlized paints can be used on their own or as highlights on work produced with other paints or mediums. Metallic paints give a super shiny feel, can be really eye catching and sparkle and gleam as on this delightful butterfly (see page 81). Pearlized paints rely on the light to reveal their true potential and often work best when applied on top of a dark background.

These paints can work really well if rubbed along the edges of craft items as a finishing touch.

Metallic leaf

Gold and silver leaf used to be the province of professionals, but with the introduction of imitation metallic leaf now we can all use it. Leaf is available in several metallic finishes and is easy to apply. You simply paint size (a special glue) over the area to be covered, press on the thin foil and rub it down, then brush away the excess. If there are gaps, just apply more size and foil until the whole area is covered. It looks very stylish and expensive, works well as a highlight or for a name or number on a card and it looks wonderful on three-dimensional objects as a background. You'll find the key motif on page 58.

Don't leave size for too long before you add the gold leaf.

Crayons and pencils

Crayons and coloured pencils produce some excellent, soft broken lines. Some are watersoluble so they can be washed with water to blend and smudge like watercolours. In general, crayons give a lovely, light sketchy feel as you can see on this cherub (page 32), and are highly suitable for card making.

Watercolour and ink

Watercolour is one of the most popular mediums. Use on a proprietary watercolour paper and stretch it to avoid warping or buy pads that are pre-stretched and easier to manage than large sheets of paper. Watercolour produces a really lovely washy look as you can see in the bunny image here (see page 65). Colours should be built up gradually as you can't take them off once applied and light pencil guidelines often look quite nice if left. Inks can be applied with brushes in the same way and they produce a very vibrant, fresh look as on the balloons, that gives colours a translucent quality. Ink looks good with a key line or outline around the image.

When using ink, play around with colours to fuse them by letting them bleed into one another.

Project gallery

These days you can buy paints suitable for decorating just about anything, so when thinking about making a gift to commemorate a special occasion it pays to think beyond a simple card or picture. Here are some ideas to get you started that are all created from the motifs in this book.

confetti boxes and cones

Here the heart and flower motif from page 82 has been painted on small boxes, a party bag and home-made party cones using acrylic paints and outliner. The outliner, which is the type that is applied straight from a nozzled tube, adds a nice finishing touch. It catches the light and provides an added dimension. If you have a lot to make, use a stencil to transfer the design quickly.

wedding stationery

Using stencils is a good way to produce a repeat design, and they work especially well with simple designs as on this wedding stationery set (left). The dove from page 88 has been applied in burgundy onto a cream pearlescent card, giving a distinctive feel. Colour co-ordinated vellum and paper layered underneath the main image on the cards, and gold rings created with outliner pen along with the gold border, provide the finishing touches. The same design is shown embossed (below), which although more time consuming to make, gives fantastic results.

father's day and mother's day cards

Once again, full use has been made of specialized craft paper, in this case the rainbow paper that provides the background for our boxes containing painted images. The gold dots have been applied with an outliner and the rest of the template has been painted using acrylic paints. See page 46 for the shoe motif and page 48 for the tie.

valentine card

Always a great occasion for card making, Valentine's Day lets us go wild with hearts. Here, our templates from the Romantic Occasions chapter (see page 82) have been cut from either gold paper or pink card. A glitter glue pen has been used to apply the gold dots that add the finishing touch. Note the embossed vellum background on the card with the gold heart.

christmas card

The main body sections of the hat and mittens (see page 78) are made from red card and the white trimmings have been cut from a sheet of pearlized white glitter card and stuck on top. The completed hat and mitten have then been applied to the snow-effect background using glue pads to give a raised, three-dimensional effect. This card really shows off the wide variety of paper and card available in the shops today for the crafter and card maker.

graduation card

This motif, from page 105, is defined with outliner and given a green tone with washes of acrylic paint. Ribbon and eyelets are used to attach the motif to a larger mount cut with decorative-edged scissors. The whole thing is mounted on a card using foam craft pads to raise it from the surface. A neat ribbon bow adds a final flourish.

scrapbook box

Created to celebrate a sixtieth birthday and using the 60 template (page 59) and the lace found on page 116 along with the beaded heart and fan from pages 82 and 84 and the key from page 58, this box has been decorated to give a scrapbook feel. Gold outliner and paint have been used for the 60, as well as to add some detail to the beaded heart. The painted lace benefits from the addition of raised highlights applied with a silver outliner pen.

folding storage tidy

The dress motif from page 31 is the inspiration for this fabric project. Using the basic shape and template, a three-dimensional image has been created, with line detail replaced by sequins and beads. The coat hanger has been made with craft wire, which easily bends into shape. These wires come in a variety of gauges and colours and are very useful for card making and other craft requirements. (The rabbit shown on page 15 is painted on the other side of the storage tidy.)

glass sun catcher

Here two Christmas motifs (see pages 78 and 79) have been successfully combined: the square with star has been enlarged to fit the item and the reindeer was then centred over the top. Glass outliner has been used to trace the templates and to provide the areas for painting. This has been done with glass paints and, to give the frosted effect the paint was applied by 'swirling' the brush onto the glass, rather than using normal brush strokes.

beaded picture frame

By using iridescent turquoise material, an old picture frame has been given a new lease of life (see right). It has been decorated with beads, which define the butterfly motif from page 81.

halloween tea-light holders

Boldly painted in bright orange, these tea-light holders have been decorated with images from the Celebrate the Year chapter (pages 70–71).

Treat candles with caution and never leave them burning unattended.

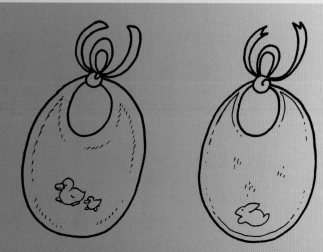

the
templates

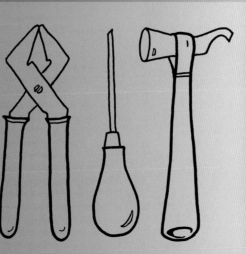

Early Years

A child's early years are such a new and exciting time that we delight in celebrating each momentous occasion with cards, gifts and encouragement. Every 'first', whether it is their first word, step or day at school, is a moment to record and look back on with fondness and pride. Memories are to be treasured, and what better way to capture the moment and celebrate it than with a handcrafted greetings card or keepsake?

The motifs in this chapter range from newborn baby images, ideal for celebrating a birth or christening, right through to children's birthdays and exam successes. No matter what the occasion, there is something to help every crafter mark their little one's milestones.

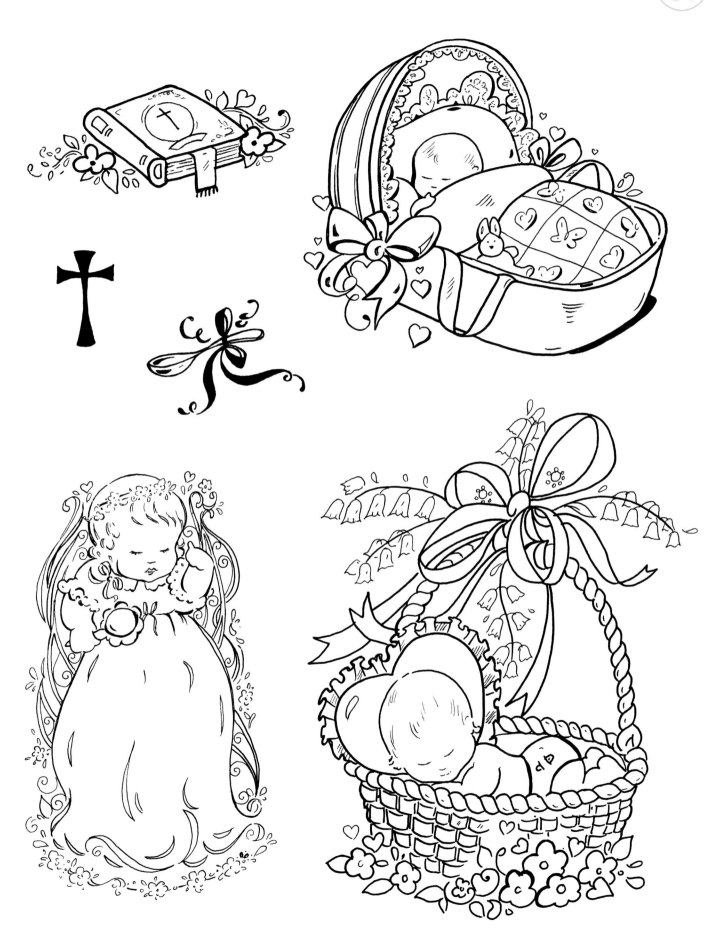

Family and Friends

Family and friends are at the heart of any celebration and in many ways just being together is a celebration in itself. But of course we want to make tokens of our appreciation and support, so this section is filled with images to help you do that.

Close friends are really part of the family, so the images here are family orientated, starting with some very simple general images that would be ideal for parties or thank-you cards. Then, because teenagers can be so hard to cater for, this group has its own section followed by motifs for ladies and more just for men. Grandparents are included too, and there's a section for sporting activities, the signs of the zodiac and significant numbers for those special birthdays and anniversaries. All in all you'll find a good basis for the decorations needed to mark any family occasion.

Celebrate the Year

People love to find a reason to celebrate, especially in the winter months when we tend to spend more time indoors and the nights are longer, darker and colder. To compensate we have plenty of annual festivals over this period that give us an excuse to decorate our homes with colour and to make merry.

The year starts with a bang, when we celebrate the first minutes of the New Year with fireworks and popping corks. These images and more are given opposite. Chinese New Year follows on and we can all celebrate with our own special animal motif. As spring warms the landscape we celebrate renewal at Easter and there are plenty of lovely images on pages 64–67 for your Easter cards and presents. In the warm days of summer the life and growth around us are celebrations in themselves, and at the end of a good summer we can give thanks for a successful harvest (pages 68-69).

As winter fast approaches there are plenty of reasons to be cheerful, starting with Halloween, then Bonfire Night and Thanksgiving. There's Diwali too, Hanukkah and Christmas and then the whole thing begins all over again.

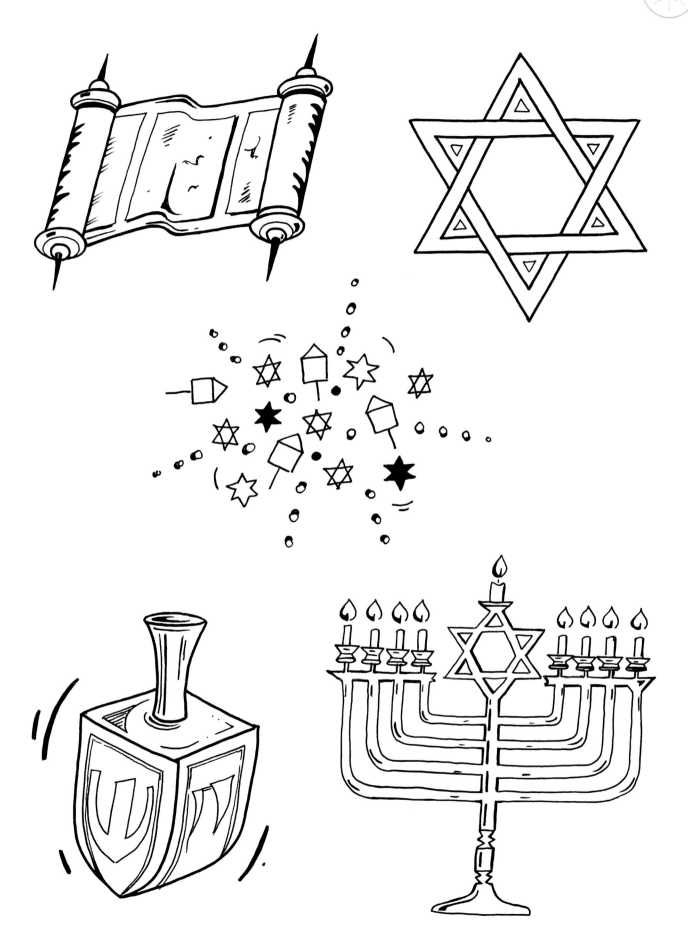

Romantic Occasions

There are reasons to be romantic every year: on anniversaries and, of course, Valentine's Day. However, there is no need to be stingy with your romantic feelings. In fact a loving gesture made out of the blue is more valuable than gold, especially if you make it clear that no reciprocal undertaking is required. Show you care just because you do, not because it is the done thing.

This chapter begins with a flourish of butterflies, the Chinese symbol of conjugal bliss and joy. Hearts and flowers follow, which are ideal for Valentine's Day decorations, and after this there are motifs for engagements, weddings and anniversaries. As with all the motifs in this book, let your imagination dictate your choice and combine several as needed to produce a unique card that says it all.

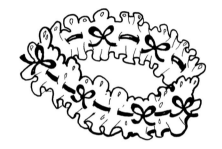

Congratulations

All of us like to feel that other people have noticed our achievements and are proud of us. With children we are ready to heap praise and applause on every success, knowing how encouraging and rewarding this is, but as we get older the acknowledgements for our successes tend to become fewer. It seems that adults are embarrassed to clap an older person on the back and say 'well done'. But everyone likes to be acknowledged and we should really take every opportunity to show our appreciation of those we love.

Show that you are thinking of a loved-one by sending a good-luck greeting before an exam using the motifs opposite. If friends are going on holiday or moving home wish them all the best with the motifs that follow. Acknowledge a new driver's licence or job, a retirement, academic or sporting achievements. All of these things show how much you care.

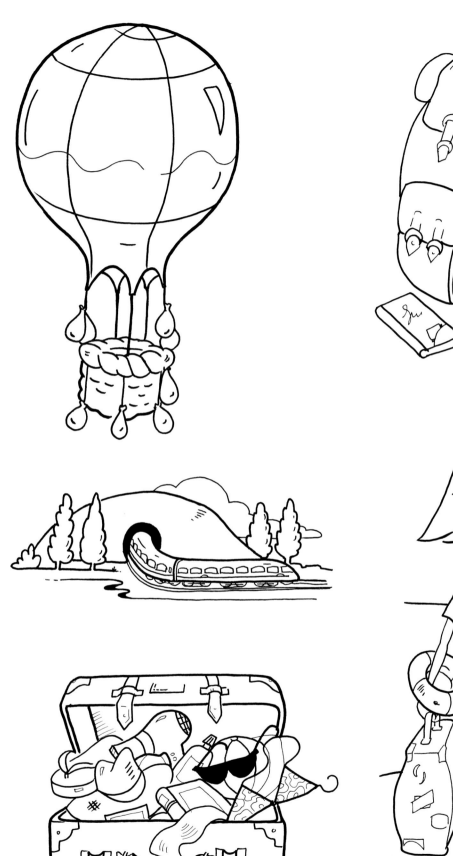

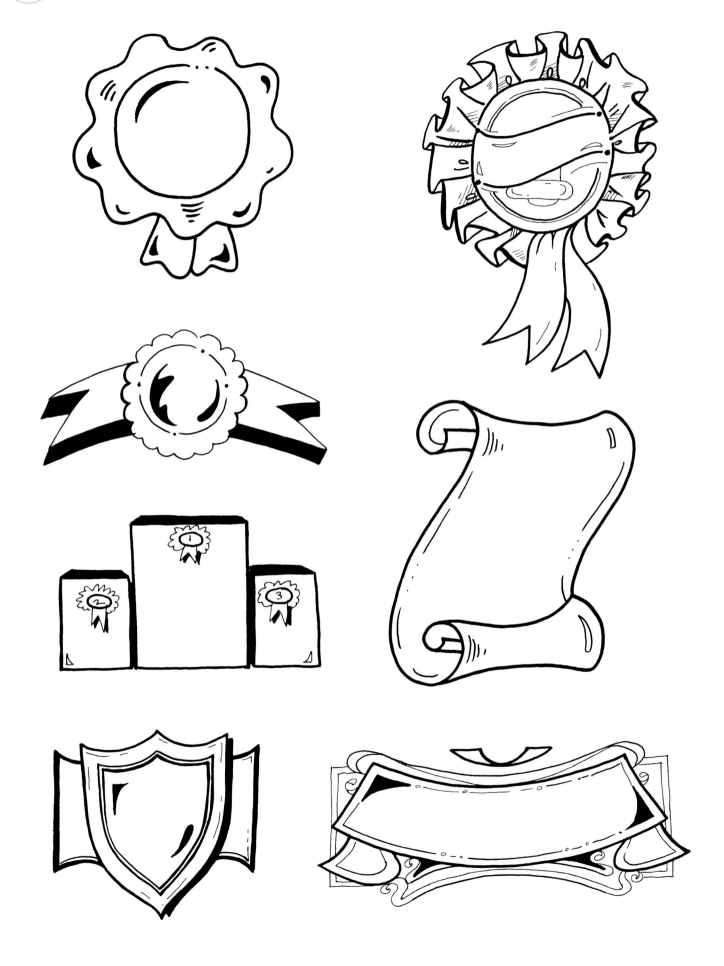

Finishing Touches

A border gives any design a professional finish and can help to draw the eye in, so this important section may turn out to be the one you rely on most. There's plenty to choose from, including elegant geometrical designs such as those shown opposite and complex flourishes that would suit a more feminine, delicate design, so you should find the perfect complement to your main motif.

Borders can also be combined with each other to make an abstract image. For example, you could use one element from any of the borders opposite as the centrepiece of a design, with one or more different borders around it. You can also use borders to focus attention on the wording of a card or even use them to finish a freehand drawing. You can use incomplete borders too, perhaps to underline a motif or to fill the empty corners of a picture. The possibilities are limited only by your imagination.

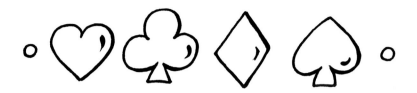

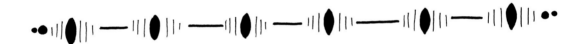

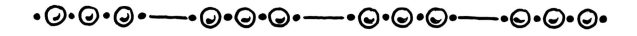

Aa Bb Cc Dd

Ee Mm Ff

Gg Hh

Ii Jj Kk Ll

Nn Oo Pp Qq

Rr Ss Tt

Uu Vv

Ww Xx Yy Zz

Index

academic achievement 104–5
acorns 75
aeroplane 96
alphabet 118–19
anniversaries 92–3
armchair 102

babies
    first time events 34–5
    new baby 29–33
baby clothes 31
baby's bottle 29
balloons 36, 43, 84
    hot-air 97
barbecue/food 55
baseball bat/glove/cap 49
bat (mammal) 70
bath 46
beehive 55
bells 89
belt, leather 92
bibs 30, 35
birdhouse 98
birds 36, 99
birthdays
    first 35
    numbers 40–1
    special numbers 58–9
bon voyage 96–7
Bonfire Night 72–3
books 33, 70, 89, 103, 104
borders 109–17
boxing glove 54
boys 50
    ill in bed 52
    schoolboy 38
    teenager 45
bread 68
breakfast tray 47
briefcase 101
bronze statuette 92
brush/comb 30
butterflies 81

cakes 35, 50, 88
candle 79
cars/motorcycles 100
cats 43, 70, 95, 104

cauldron 71
CDs (compact discs) 45
certificates 106, 107
champagne bottle 61, 86
chess pieces 54
chickens/eggs 64
chicks 64
Chinese New Year 62–3
chocolates 85
christenings 39
Christmas 35, 78–9
churches 39, 89
clocks/watches 61, 102
collar and tie 38, 48
comb/brush 30
computer 101
confetti 89
corn 68, 74
cornucopia 75
cot/baby 31, 33
cotton reel 92
crib/twins 32
cricket bat/stumps 49
cricketer 49
crosses 33, 39
Cupid 85
cups & rosettes 106–7

desert island 96
diamonds 86, 87, 93
diplomas 105
divas 76
Diwali 76
doll 36
door/porch 99
doves 39, 88
draughtboard 54
dreidles 39, 77
dresses 46, 90
driving success 100
duckling 37

Easter 64–7
eggs 64, 66
    Easter eggs 66, 67
elephant 104
engagements 86–7
eyes 70

fairy 44
Father's Day 48–9
fields 68
fingers, crossed 95
fireworks 61, 72–3
fishing rod 54
flowers 44, 46, 47, 51, 53, 82–5, 91
    spring flowers 67
football 49, 54
footprints 96
fruit 52, 69

garden
    assorted objects 51
    tools 103
garter 90
gate 99
general images 43
getting better 52
ghost 71
gifts 35, 43, 50, 79, 84, 91
girls
    schoolgirl 38
    teenager 44
glasses, drinking 61, 86, 93
gold bars 93
golf club/ball & tee 51
good luck 95
grandparents 51
greetings cards 47
Guy Fawkes 73

Halloween 70–1
hammock 103
handbag 44
hannukiah 39, 77
Hanukkah 77
hare 65
Harvest Festival 68–9
hats 48–9, 55, 67, 71, 90, 105
hearts 44, 82–5, 86, 87, 88, 91
hobbies & sports 54–5
holidaymaker 97
horse and jockey 54
horseshoes 89, 95
hot water bottle 52
household possessions 98
houses 71, 98–9

ice cream 37
injured man 52

keys 29, 58, 59, 100
knitting wool 51

L plate 100
lace 93
lamb 65
letter box/letters 98
lighthouse 96
linen sheets 92

magic wand 95
mermaid/dolphin 50
mobile phone 45
moon and star 76
Mother's Day 46–7

nappies 29
Nature's bounty 69, 75
new home 98–9
new job 101
New Year 61

palette/brush 55
paper 92
pearl 93
pens/pencils 38, 101, 104
piano keys 93
Pilgrim 74
pocket calculator 104

prams 32
pumpkin 70, 75

rabbits 65
radio cassette 45
rainbow/crock of gold 95
rattle, baby's 30
reindeer 35, 79
religion 39
removal van 98
retirement 102–3
rings 87, 88, 93
rosettes & cups 106–7
rucksack 97
rugby ball 49

safety pins 30
Santa Claus 79
saucepan 93
school, starting 35, 38
schoolhouse 38
shamrock 95
shell 96
ships 54, 96, 102
shoes 34, 46, 50
shopping 46
skateboarder 45
skull 71
sleigh 79
snowman 78
soother, baby's 29
spider/web 70
spoons 33, 92

sports & hobbies 54–5
stars 77, 78
stork/baby 30
suitcase 97

teapot 93
teddy bear 35, 36, 53
telephone 101
tenpin bowls 55
thank you 53
Thanksgiving 74–5
tiara 90
toddlers 36–7
tools 48
Torah 39, 77
toys 29, 31, 36, 37
traffic lights 100
train/tunnel 97
tree 103
    Christmas 78
turkeys 74

Valentine's Day 82–5
vase 92

wedding outfits 90
weddings 88–91
witch/broomstick 71
wrought iron 92

youngsters 50

zodiac signs 56–7

About the author

Sharon Bennett studied graphics and illustration at college before embarking upon a successful career as a packaging designer for various consultancies, eventually becoming Senior Designer for a major confectionery company. In 1986 she started working on a freelance basis in order to divide her time between work and bringing up her family. It was during this time that she moved into the craft world and began to contribute projects to national UK magazines such as *Crafts Beautiful*, and worked on their craft booklets. Sharon has produced two other books in this series for David & Charles, *The Crafter's Design Library: Christmas* and *The Crafter's Design Library: Florals*. Sharon lives with her family in Essex, UK.